flavoring with
Herbs

flavoring with

Herbs

Clare Gordon-Smith

photography by

James Merrell

RYLAND
PETERS
& SMALL

Art Director **Jacqui Small**

Art Editor **Penny Stock**

Design Assistant **Lucy Hamilton**

Editor **Elsa Petersen-Schepelern**

Photography **James Merrell**

Food Stylist **Clare Gordon-Smith**

Stylist **Wei Tang**

Production Manager **Kate Mackillop**

Our thanks to Christine Walsh, Ian Bartlett and Poppy Gordon-Smith

First published in the USA in 1997
This edition published in 2000 by
Ryland Peters & Small
Cavendish House
51–55 Mortimer Street, London W1N 7TD

10 9 8 7 6 5 4 3 2 1

Notes:
Ovens should be preheated to the specified temperature. If using a convection oven, adjust time and temperature according to the manufacturer's instructions.

ISBN 1-8-4172-066-6

A CIP catalog record for this book is available from the Library of Congress.

Herbs have been used through history for both cooking and medicinal purposes. Traditional herbs—parsley, sage, rosemary, and thyme—have been joined by other favorites, such as tarragon, basil, mint, dill, bay leaf, oregano, chives, and chervil, forming an eclectic mix of flavoring ingredients. Modern-day cooks also use herbs from the cuisines of China, India, and Southeast Asia. Widely available in small shops and supermarkets—sold either in bunches or growing in little pots—fresh herbs are now within everyone's reach.

Shown here (back row, from left) is a small bay tree, providing bay leaves, one of the most traditional herbs, an infusion of herbs in red wine vinegar, and lavender-flavored sugar, which is used in baking.

Front row, from left, is a bundle of **Asian herbs**, now widely used in modern cooking, consisting of lemon grass, kaffir lime leaves, and cilantro; a hot infusion of herbs in olive oil makes a quick dressing for a warm salad, or a nice flavoring sprinkled over boiled or roasted vegetables. Shown far right is one of the best of all herb flavorings—**pesto**, usually made with basil, garlic, pignoli nuts, and olive oil. Inspired chefs have made innovative changes, using arugula, parsley, or even cilantro instead of basil, to give more unusual flavors.

the flavors of

Herbs

Marjoram **Oregano** **Basil** **Thyme** **Chervil** **Lavender**

Mint **Lemon thyme** **Rosemary** **Bay leaves**

Herbs are important flavoring ingredients in all the world's great cuisines. Rosemary, thyme, and lavender grow wild in the South of France, and have been enthusiastically adopted by cooks working in the western cooking tradition. Chives, chervil, and marjoram are widely used in European cuisines. Oregano is

marjoram's wild cousin, and is typically used in Greek cooking. Dill, with its feathery leaves, its close relation fennel, and curly parsley, are all traditional herbs used in Northern European cooking. Flat-leaf parsley, more commonly used in Italy, is thought to have better flavor than its crinkly cousin. Other

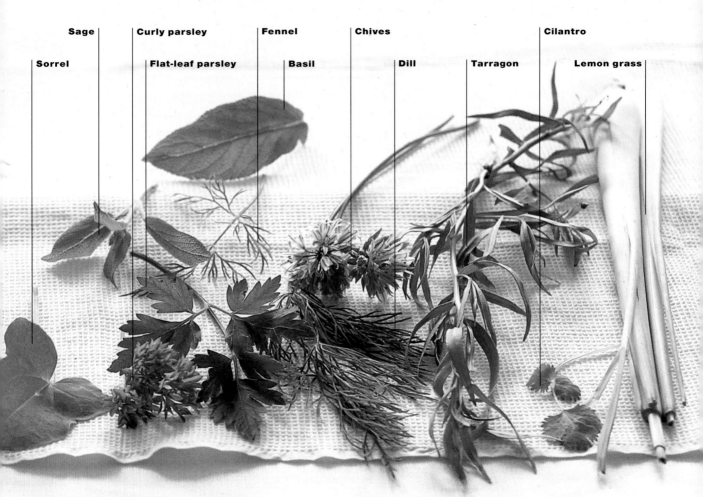

Sage | Curly parsley | Fennel | Chives | Cilantro

Sorrel | Flat-leaf parsley | Basil | Dill | Tarragon | Lemon grass

Italian favorites are sweet basil and tarragon. Of the hundreds of different varieties of mint, the most widely used are spearmint and the peppery-tasting Asian mint. They are part of traditional cuisines ranging from Europe to the Middle East, India, and Southeast Asia—and in the mint juleps of Kentucky. Cilantro is used in Vietnam, Latin America, the Caribbean, and Thailand, which also uses lemon grass. Though dried herbs are traditional in some dishes, such as lasagne, fresh herbs have been used throughout this book for better flavor. If using dried herbs, use half the quantities given for fresh ones.

The flavors of herbs **9**

Appetizers

Sweet potato soup
with chive mascarpone cream

Sweet potatoes produce a soup with wonderful color, sweet flavor, and dense texture. This one is topped with chive cream, and you could use purple chive flowers to garnish, if available. Chives are great for people who don't have room for a garden—plant them in small terra-cotta pots and set out on the terrace, or even on a window sill. Cut off the leaves close to the roots—the more you cut, the stronger they grow. The dish will look better if you snip up the leaves with scissors rather than using a knife.

Heat the olive oil in a skillet, add the shallots and garlic, and sauté gently until softened. Stir in the sweet potatoes, carrots, and thyme. Cover the skillet and cook the vegetables for 4 minutes. Stir in the chicken stock and apple juice, bring to a gentle boil and simmer for 20 to 30 minutes until just soft and tender. Transfer to a blender or food processor, and puree until smooth. Return the soup to a clean skillet or saucepan, taste and adjust the seasoning, then reheat gently.

To make the chive cream, mix the snipped chives and flat-leaf parsley into the mascarpone and season to taste. Pour the soup into heated soup bowls, place a spoonful of chive cream on each one, then add the chive flowers, if using.

Serve with herbed bread rolls or bread sticks.

1 tablespoon olive oil

2 shallots, finely chopped

1 garlic clove, crushed

1 lb. sweet potatoes, cubed

4 oz. carrots

2 tablespoons chopped fresh lemon thyme leaves

2½ cups chicken stock

⅔ cup apple juice

chive flowers, to serve (optional)

chive mascarpone cream

2 tablespoon snipped fresh chives

1 tablespoon chopped fresh flat-leaf parsley

5 tablespoons mascarpone

salt and freshly ground black pepper

Serves 4

Couscous salad
with cilantro and shrimp

Thai fish sauce is available in gourmet shops or larger supermarkets.

Diagonally slice the beans, scallions, and cucumber, place in a bowl, sprinkle with the vinegar, and leave for 10 minutes. Reserve half the cucumber. Bruise the lemon grass by tapping firmly with a rolling pin or the flat of a heavy knife, then place in a bowl with the couscous and fish sauce. Pour over 1¼ cups boiling water and soak for 10 minutes. Chop the herbs and mix with the vegetables and couscous. Remove the lemon grass, pack the mixture into small glasses. Serve with accompaniments such as arugula leaves, the reserved cucumber, and shrimp, if using.

8 oz. green beans

1 bunch of scallions

1 cucumber, peeled and seeded

2 tablespoons vinegar

1 stalk of lemon grass

6 oz. couscous

1 tablespoon fish sauce

1 bunch of cilantro

1 bunch of mint

arugula leaves

4 oz. shrimp (optional)

Serves 4

Fresh crab salad
with lemon chervil vinaigrette

Chervil is a member of the parsley family, with a delicately pretty, feathery leaf. Use cider vinegar or rice vinegar in this recipe.

Mix the chervil, olive oil, vinegar, and honey in a bowl. Stir in the crabmeat, tomatoes, and cucumber. Pack into small cups, place on the plates, and serve with accompaniments such as toasted baguette and mixed salad leaves.

2 tablespoons chopped fresh chervil leaves

6 tablespoons olive oil

1 tablespoon vinegar

2 teaspoons honey

8 oz. crabmeat

4 oz. cherry tomatoes, chopped

1 cucumber, chopped

Serves 4

Cucumber mousse
with dill and mixed herb salad

Dill has a mild aniseed taste that marries
well with other cool ingredients like
cucumbers and crème fraîche. This recipe
from *Marie Claire* magazine is light and airy—
ideal as a starter, or as an accompaniment
for smoked fish. You needn't buy special
mousse molds—just set them in chunky
French bistro-style cups or tumblers.

Chop the cucumbers into 2-inch pieces. Place in a
pan, just cover with water, bring to a boil, simmer for
about 3 minutes until soft, then drain.
Place in a blender or food processor, puree for about
1 minute until smooth, then transfer to a bowl. Stir in
the crème fraîche, dill, watercress, scallions, and
lemon zest, then salt, pepper, and lemon juice.
Dissolve the gelatin in a little water, according to the
package instructions, and fold into the mousse.
Spoon the mixture into 6 molds or tumblers.
Chill for about 2 hours.
Serve with a light herb salad and a vinaigrette.

3 large cucumbers,
peeled, halved,
and seeded

1¼ cups crème fraîche

1½ tablespoons
chopped fresh dill

2 oz. watercress,
finely chopped

4 scallions,
finely chopped

grated zest and
juice of ½ lemon

1½ packets gelatin

sea salt and freshly
ground black pepper

herb salad with
vinaigrette, to serve

Serves 4

roasted tomatoes have a **heavenly and intense** flavor

that marries well with fresh **basil and oregano**

Basil custard phyllo pies
with oregano and roasted tomatoes

Roasting plum tomatoes gives the most heavenly and intense flavor. Oregano is a wild marjoram used widely in Greek and Italian cooking, especially with tomatoes. Like most herbs, it's better used fresh, but if you find the big bunches of dried oregano sold in Greek delicatessens, buy some, if only to make your kitchen smell marvelous.

Place the tomatoes on a baking tray, dab with olive oil, sprinkle with oregano, sea salt, and black pepper. Place in a preheated oven and roast at 400°F for about 15 to 20 minutes.

To make the phyllo pie shells, melt the butter and stir in the oregano. Using a pair of scissors, cut the pastry into sixteen 6-inch squares.

Brush four 4-inch pie dishes with the oregano-flavored butter, then layer 4 sheets of pastry into each dish, brushing each layer with herb butter. Cover with foil and bake at 400°F for 10 to 15 minutes until just golden. Remove from the oven and reduce the temperature to 300°F.

Beat the custard ingredients together, then spoon the mixture into the pie shells.

Return to the oven and cook for 20 to 30 minutes until just set. Place the roasted tomatoes on top and cook for a further 10 minutes.

Serve warm with a salad of herbs and mustard greens, and a herb vinaigrette.

1 lb. plum tomatoes, cut in half

1 tablespoon olive oil

2 tablespoons chopped fresh oregano leaves

sea salt and freshly ground black pepper

herbed phyllo pastry

4 tablespoons butter

1 tablespoon snipped fresh oregano leaves

8 sheets of phyllo pastry

basil custard

1 egg

⅔ cup heavy cream

3 tablespoons chopped fresh basil leaves

to serve

salad of mustard greens and assorted herbs

herb vinaigrette

Serves 4

Summer vegetables
with a caper and parsley sauce

Usually teamed with carpaccio—thinly sliced Italian raw beef—this sauce is also good with vegetarian dishes. Don't think parsley is ordinary because it's familiar—it's a great basic flavoring, with a fresh, clean taste.

2 bulbs of baby fennel

2 zucchini

4 plum tomatoes

4 large scallions

caper and parsley sauce

4 tablespoons white wine vinegar

6 gherkins or cornichons

4 tablespoons chopped fresh flat-leaf parsley

2 garlic cloves

2 anchovy fillets

3 tablespoons capers

1 onion, chopped

¾ cup olive oil

Serves 4

Slice all the vegetables in half lengthwise and arrange on a serving platter.

Place all the sauce ingredients, except the olive oil, in a blender or food processor, and puree. With the machine still running, add the oil drop by drop to make a thick green sauce.

Chill until ready to serve.

Alternatively, roast a selection of vegetables in a preheated oven at 400°F for about 20 minutes, or until crispy at the edges, then serve warm with the caper and parsley sauce.

Herbed risotto cakes
with crispy spinach and sage

Risotto is a popular dish—and substantial enough to serve as a main course for lunch. But it also makes an interesting appetizer in smaller portions, as in these timbales. Deep-fried herb leaves make a wonderful garnish idea. You could also make fries from vegetables such as sweet potatoes or parsnips—a little tricky to prepare, but worth the trouble for a special occasion.

To make the risotto, melt the butter and olive oil in a skillet, add the shallots and gently sauté until soft and tender. Stir in the rice and garlic, cook gently for a few minutes, then stir in the hot stock, one ladle at a time, waiting until each ladleful has been absorbed, before adding the next. Stir in the herbs, then press the rice into 4 molds or cups, and keep them warm while you prepare the crispy spinach and sage leaves.

Heat the corn oil in a deep-fryer or saucepan to 350°F, or until a cube of bread browns in 30 seconds. Add the spinach leaves, and fry for a few minutes until crisp and tender, then remove and drain on paper towels. Repeat with the sage leaves. Invert the risotto cakes onto appetizer plates, then serve with the crispy leaves.

2 tablespoons butter

1 tablespoon olive oil

2 shallots, finely chopped

1 cup risotto rice, plus 1 tablespoon

1 garlic clove, crushed

1½ cups hot chicken stock

2 tablespoons chopped fresh lemon thyme leaves

1 tablespoon chopped fresh sage leaves

sea salt

crispy spinach and sage leaves

corn oil, for frying

2 oz. spinach leaves

handful of sage leaves

Serves 4

deep-fried **crispy herb leaves** make an unusual garnish

Fish

Breaded mussels
with chives and sage

Sage has a strong, rather smoky taste, which marries well with the assertive flavors of mussels. This recipe is based on an Italian original, in which Italian sausage is mixed with sage then used to fill the mussels. The shells are then trussed up with chive leaves and baked. You could also make a simpler dish by just mixing the breadcrumbs with a little pesto and lemon juice.

1 bunch of fresh chives

1½ lb. mussels, cleaned

2 tablespoons white wine

2 tablespoons extra-virgin olive oil

2 garlic cloves, crushed

2 oz. fresh Italian pork sausage, skins removed

1 cup dried breadcrumbs

about 30 fresh sage leaves

salt and freshly ground black pepper

to serve

lemon wedges

crusty bread

Serves 4

Blanch the chives in boiling water for 1 minute. Drain and run under cold water. This will make them pliable enough to tie up the packages.

Place the mussels in a dry skillet just large enough to hold them, then add the white wine. Cover the skillet and cook over high heat for 2 to 3 minutes until the shells are just open.

Heat half the oil in another skillet and, when hot, add the garlic and sauté gently. Crumble the sausage and add to the pan, then add the breadcrumbs. Season with freshly ground black pepper.

Place a small amount of the breadcrumb mixture inside each mussel and top with a sage leaf. Close the shells and tie each one with a blanched chive. Place the remaining olive oil in a roasting pan, add the mussels and cook in a preheated oven at 375°F for 12 to 15 minutes. Serve with lemon wedges and lots of crusty bread.

Salmon with fennel
on mint tabbouleh salad

A recipe that's been given the Pacific Rim
treatment, with a mixture of flavors and
culinary influences. Lebanese tabbouleh
salad is usually made with bulgar wheat—but
it's also wonderful made with couscous, that
staple of North African cooking. The pretty
fronds of fennel are perfect with salmon.
Fennel is easy to grow in the garden—and
there is a beautiful bronze variety that tastes
as wonderful as it looks. If you can't find the
true fennel herb, you could also use the
feathery fronds of fennel bulbs—or dill.

Place the couscous in a bowl, pour over 1¼ cups
boiling water, and set aside for 10 minutes.
Place the salmon and asparagus in a roasting pan.
Brush both with olive oil, season with salt, and
sprinkle with parsley. Cook in a preheated oven at
400°F for 5 to 7 minutes.
Finely slice the scallions and tear the mint leaves
into pieces. Fluff up the couscous with a fork, then
stir in the scallions and mint.
Place a spoonful of couscous tabbouleh on each
plate, arrange the asparagus and pickled ginger on
top, then add the roasted salmon.
Mix the fennel dressing ingredients together,
sprinkle over the salmon and tabbouleh, then serve.
Tie up the asparagus with chive flowers and add
fennel sprigs, if using.

6 oz. couscous

4 slices of salmon fillet,
about 2 inches wide

8 oz. asparagus
spears, trimmed

2 tablespoons olive oil

2 tablespoons chopped
fresh flat-leaf parsley

1 bunch of scallions

1 bunch of fresh mint

2 tablespoons
pickled pink ginger
(from Asian food stores)

salt

fennel dressing

4 tablespoons chopped
fresh fennel leaves

1 tablespoon honey

4 tablespoons olive oil

salt and freshly
ground black pepper

to serve

sprigs of fennel

chive flowers (optional)

Serves 4

Pan-fried monkfish
with chermoula marinade

Chermoula is a spicy cilantro and parsley marinade from Morocco—great with monkfish, which is firm enough to hold its shape, while still absorbing all the spicy flavors. Stir-fried vegetables or steamed coconut rice would make an interesting multi-cultural accompaniment to this dish.

1 lb. monkfish tail, skinned and boned

2 tablespoon olive oil

chermoula

1 bunch of cilantro

1 bunch of parsley

2 garlic cloves, crushed

1 teaspoon ground cumin

1 teaspoon ground paprika

juice of 2 lemons

grated rind of 1 lemon

2 tablespoons olive oil

Serves 4

To make the chermoula, chop all the herbs together using a sharp knife. Place in a bowl, mix in the garlic, cumin, paprika, lemon juice and grated zest, and stir in the olive oil.

Cut the monkfish into slices and place in a shallow dish. Spoon over the chermoula and place in the refrigerator to marinate for at least 30 minutes, or up to 4 hours.

Heat the olive oil in a skillet, remove the fish from the marinade and gently sauté it for about 4 minutes on each side. Meanwhile, pour the marinade into a pan and heat gently. To serve, place the fish on heated plates and drizzle over the marinade.

Thai sea bass with
ginger and lemon grass glaze

Sea bass is ideal for this dish, but you could
also use halibut or cod. Lemon grass, one of
the major flavoring ingredients of Thai and
Vietnamese cooking, is a relatively new
addition to our herb repertoire. It is widely
available, but if you can't find it on the same
day as you buy the fish, you could double the
quantity of lemon juice instead, though the
flavor would not be quite the same.

Mix the glaze ingredients together, place the fish in a
shallow dish, pour over the marinade, and chill for at
least 30 minutes, or up to 2 hours.
Remove the fish from the marinade and place on a
preheated cast-iron stove-top grill, brush with the
marinade, and cook for about 3 minutes in total.
Heat the oil in a wok or skillet, add the scallions,
chile, sugar snap and snow peas, and quickly stir-fry.
Meanwhile, gently heat the remaining glaze in a
saucepan. To serve, place the fish on heated plates,
add the vegetables, drizzle with the glaze, and
garnish with sprigs of cilantro.

1 lb. sea bass, halibut
steaks, or cod

1 tablespoon corn oil

1 bunch of scallions

1 red chile, seeded,
and finely sliced

6 oz. sugar snap peas

6 oz. snow peas

sprigs of cilantro,
to serve

lemon grass glaze

1 tablespoon light
brown sugar

1 tablespoon
light soy sauce

1 tablespoon
lemon juice

2 tablespoons sherry

2 stalks of fresh
lemon grass, bruised

1-inch piece of fresh
ginger, peeled, and
finely diced

1 garlic clove, crushed

Serves 4

Thai-style fish and fries
with cilantro dipping sauce

Classic British fish and chips (fries) are given a modern update with a Thai twist via the cilantro—a favorite herb in Southeast Asian cooking. Use cod or sole for this dish, and serve with sweet potato fries. Fries are always better when twice-cooked. Deep-fry them first until golden, drain, cool a little, then fry again until light brown and crisp. Made with sweet potato, they're even better than with ordinary potato.

To make the fries, peel the sweet potatoes and cut into thin slices. Rinse under cold running water and pat dry. Heat the oil in a deep-fryer or saucepan to about 350°F, or until a cube of bread browns in 30 seconds. Add the sweet potato and fry until golden. Set aside to keep warm.

Cut the fish into strips. To make the batter, beat the egg white with the salt, then fold in the sesame seeds. Dip the fish first into cornstarch, then into the sesame and egg white batter.

Heat the oil in a wok or skillet to about 350°F. Add the pieces of fish and gently sauté for about 7 to 10 minutes until just golden. Meanwhile, reheat the oil in the deep-fryer, add the sweet potato, and cook for a second time until brown and crispy. Drain and sprinkle with sea salt. Mix together the dipping sauce ingredients, and serve with the fish and fries.

1 lb. fish fillets

oil, for pan-frying

sesame batter

1 large egg white

a pinch of salt

1 tablespoon cornstarch

2 tablespoons white
sesame seeds

fries

1 lb. sweet potatoes

peanut oil, or corn oil,
for deep-frying

sea salt

dipping sauce

3 tablespoons pickled
ginger juice (optional)

1 teaspoon sugar

1 tablespoon
rice vinegar

2–3 tablespoons
chopped fresh
cilantro leaves

1 red chile, seeded
and chopped

2 tablespoons soy sauce

Serves 4

Meat and poultry

Duck breast salad
with cilantro and lemon grass

Lemon grass with cilantro is a wonderful marriage of flavors, giving a fresh, clean taste. Mix them with other Thai-influenced ingredients to give a truly wonderful dish.

Mix the marinade ingredients together, add the duck breasts, and set aside to marinate in the refrigerator for up to 24 hours.

Remove the duck breasts from the marinade, place in a roasting pan, brush with honey, and sprinkle with the sesame seeds. Cook in a preheated oven at 400°F for 20 minutes. Remove from the oven, set them aside to rest for 5 minutes, then slice.

Soak the noodles in boiling water for 3 minutes, or according to the package instructions, then drain. Heat the marinade in a small pan, then pour over the cooked noodles. Mix the scallions and bean sprouts into the noodles.

To serve, place the watercress on heated plates, add a pile of noodles and a few slices of the duck breasts, and sprinkle with fresh basil leaves, if using.

2–4 duck breasts

1 teaspoon honey

1 tablespoon sesame seeds

1 package Chinese or Thai dried egg noodles

1 bunch of scallions, sliced diagonally

3 cups bean sprouts

4 oz. watercress

fresh basil leaves, or Asian basil (optional)

lemon grass marinade

1 tablespoon honey

1 tablespoon Thai fish sauce

2 tablespoon sherry

1 garlic clove, crushed

2 stalks lemon grass, crushed

1 tablespoon fresh cilantro, roughly chopped

Serves 4

Tarragon chicken
with herbed crème fraîche sauce

Chicken and tarragon form one of the classic combinations, especially in French cooking. Tarragon has a strong, peppery taste, that is also wonderful in pizzas—the Italians rather romantically call it *dragoncello*.

Place the chicken in a casserole dish with the tarragon, parsley, water, and seasoning, bring to a gentle simmer, and poach for about 20 minutes, or until tender. Allow to cool slightly in the poaching liquid. Remove the chicken from the dish, and reserve the poaching liquid to use as stock. Using a knife, slice the meat away from the bones, keeping the pieces large and chunky. Heat the olive oil in the casserole dish, and lightly sauté the shallots until softened and transparent. Stir in the flour and cook for 1 minute, to allow the starch grains to burst. Remove from the heat, gradually stir in the reserved stock, little by little, to prevent lumps forming. Return to the heat, bring to a boil, and simmer for 1 minute. Stir in the crème fraîche, then add the chicken and chopped herbs. To make the sautéed potatoes, heat the butter and oil in a skillet, and cook the potatoes until golden. Serve with with the chicken and sprinkle with sprigs of parsley and tarragon.

4 chicken pieces

4 sprigs of tarragon, plus extra to serve

2 sprigs of curly parsley, plus extra to serve

1 cup water

1 tablespoon olive oil

2 shallots, sliced

1 tablespoon all-purpose flour

1 cup low-fat crème fraîche

1 teaspoon chopped fresh tarragon

1 tablespoon chopped fresh parsley

salt and freshly ground black pepper

sprigs of parsley and tarragon, to serve

sautéed potatoes

2 tablespoons butter

1 tablespoon olive oil

1 lb. potatoes, thinly sliced

Serves 4

Chicken breasts
with sorrel, chives, and mascarpone

Chicken—low-fat and versatile—is still the
most popular meat in the world. You could
also replace it with turkey in this recipe—
both chicken and turkey are perfect with the
light, gentle flavors of herbs. Sorrel is easy
to grow in the garden, or even in a window
box, and is also available through gourmet
shops and larger supermarkets. If it is
unavailable, use baby spinach instead.

4 chicken breasts,
skin and bone removed,
or turkey escalopes

8 oz. fresh sorrel

3 tablespoons
snipped chives

4 oz. mascarpone

olive oil, for roasting

sea salt and freshly
ground black pepper

cooked fresh pasta,
to serve

Serves 4

Place the chicken breasts, cut sides up, between two
sheets of waxed paper on a board. Using a wooden
rolling pin, hit hard to flatten the breasts to a thinner
and more even texture.
Place the sorrel leaves on top of the breasts. Mix the
chives into the mascarpone, and season with salt and
pepper. Add 1 tablespoon to each breast, on top of
the sorrel, and spread out. Roll up into parcels and
secure with cocktail sticks.
Place in a roasting pan, drizzle with a little olive oil,
sprinkle with sea salt and black pepper, and cook in
a preheated oven at 400°F for 20 to 30 minutes.
Serve with fresh pasta made with wild garlic, or plain
pasta tossed in parsley pesto.

Pork and lime brochettes
with lemon grass marinade

The wonderful, heady flavors of Thai cuisine,
with wafts of lemon grass, kaffir lime leaves,
and coconut, marry well with chicken or
pork. Kaffir lime leaves are sold in Asian
markets—buy extra and freeze the leftovers
so you always have some on hand.

1 eggplant,
quartered and sliced

1½ lb. pork fillet, cut
into 1-inch pieces

2 limes, cut into wedges

2 kaffir lime leaves
(optional)

**lemon grass
marinade**

2 stalks of lemon grass

2 tablespoons mirin
(Japanese rice wine),
or dry sherry

4 tablespoons
coconut milk

2 sprigs of basil

1 garlic clove, crushed

Serves 4

To prepare the marinade, first cut the lemon grass in
half lengthwise and bruise by tapping firmly with a
rolling pin or the flat of a heavy knife.
Mix the marinade ingredients together, add the
eggplant and the pork, then chill for 2 to 12 hours,
depending on the time available.
When ready to cook, remove the eggplant and meat
from the marinade. Thread onto soaked wooden
skewers, alternating with wedges of lime and pieces
of kaffir lime leaves, if using.
Place the brochettes on a hot stove-top grill-pan (or
barbecue) and cook for about 7 minutes, until the
meat is thoroughly cooked.
Steamed coconut rice and a little sweet and sour
dipping sauce would be suitable accompaniments.

Vietnamese pork
stir-fried with bok choy and mint

Pork in a Pan-Pacific sauce—using flavors of tamarind mixed with spices and mint. Use hot Vietnamese mint, if you can find it, but ordinary mint—especially spearmint—is an acceptable substitute.

Mix the marinade ingredients together, add the pork, and leave to marinate for about 2 hours.
Heat half the corn oil in a skillet or wok, remove the pork from the marinade, and gently sauté. When sealed and brown, stir in the cucumber, stir-fry for a few minutes, then add the marinade, bring to a boil, and simmer for 5 to 10 minutes until thickened.
Prepare the egg noodles according to the package instructions.
Pull the bok choy apart, heat the remaining oil in a wok or skillet, and stir-fry the leaves until wilted.
Drain the noodles and serve with the bok choy and pork, sprinkled with cilantro.

1 lb. pork fillet, sliced

2 tablespoons corn oil

1 cucumber, peeled, halved lengthwise, seeded, then sliced diagonally

1 package Chinese or Thai dried egg noodles

4 small bok choy

sprigs of cilantro, to garnish

tamarind marinade

6 tablespoons tamarind paste

1 garlic clove, chopped

1 teaspoon chile powder

¼ teaspoon ground ginger

1 bunch of scallions

1 green chile, sliced

4 plum tomatoes, finely chopped

2 tablespoons torn leaves of fresh mint

⅔ cup rice vinegar

Serves 4

Pork and fennel daube
with potato and bay leaf gratin

Fennel has a gentle anise flavor, and the
seeds often form the basis of curry spice
mixes. A twist on the classic French dish,
this recipe uses all three types of fennel—
the herb, the bulb, and the seeds. The
fennel herb, especially the pretty bronze
variety, is easily grown in the garden, or you
could substitute the feathery fronds from the
top of the bulb, as shown below.

To prepare the gratin, place the sliced potatoes and
onion in a gratin dish, season with salt and pepper,
add the bay leaves and milk, and brush the top with
melted butter. Set aside until ready to cook the meat.
Heat the oil in a deep casserole dish, add the pork,
and brown on all sides. Stir in the fennel seeds,
bacon pieces, and onions. Stir in the cornstarch,
cook for 1 minute, then stir in the stock and red
wine, tomatoes, fennel pieces, and fresh bay leaves.
Place the potato gratin and the pork daube in a
preheated oven and cook at 350°F for 40 minutes.
The pork can also be simmered on top of the
stove, covered, for 50 minutes.
Serve the daube and gratin together.

1 tablespoon olive oil

1 lb. pork cut into
1-inch pieces

2 teaspoons
fennel seeds

4 slices of bacon,
chopped

3 onions, sliced

1 tablespoon cornstarch

1¼ cups chicken stock

⅓ cup red wine

4 plum tomatoes, halved

2 fennel bulbs, sliced

2 fresh bay leaves

sprigs of fennel,
to serve

**bay leaf and
potato gratin**

1 lb. potatoes,
thinly sliced

1 onion, thinly sliced

2 bay leaves

⅓ cup milk

melted butter,
for brushing

Serves 4

Lamb with thyme
and fresh mint vinaigrette

The woody scent of rosemary and thyme is reminiscent of the beautiful food and landscapes of the South of France. Lamb is traditionally combined with these herbs and also served with mint vinaigrette. Tossing steamed or boiled vegetables with herbs and butter is also traditional.

Place the lamb in a roasting pan. Using a sharp knife, cut slits into the meat and insert slices of garlic. Brush with oil, sprinkle with thyme, and cook in a preheated oven at 375°F for about 1 hour. To make the vinaigrette, mix the mint with the sugar, salt, pepper, vinegar, and olive oil, and set aside. Clean the carrots, leaving a little of the green tops intact. To clean the leeks, remove the root and trim the ragged green leaves. Slit the green part lengthwise and rinse well to remove all the sand. Scrub the potatoes and boil in salted water for 20 minutes. Steam the carrots and leeks in a steamer over the pan of potatoes, for about 10 minutes, or until just tender.
Reserve ⅔ cup of the vegetable water. Drain the vegetables and toss in chives and butter. To make the gravy, pour off the fat from the roasting pan, stir in the flour, then add the red wine and the reserved vegetable water. Boil for a few minutes, stirring, until thickened. Carve the lamb and serve with the vinaigrette, vegetables, and a little gravy.

½ leg of lamb

1 garlic clove, sliced

olive oil, for brushing

2 tablespoons chopped fresh thyme leaves

mint vinaigrette

1 large bunch of fresh mint leaves, chopped

a pinch of sugar

2 tablespoons red wine vinegar

2 tablespoons olive oil

salt and pepper

chive vegetables

8 oz. carrots

1 lb. young leeks

1 lb. new potatoes

2 tablespoons snipped fresh chives

2 tablespoons butter

red wine gravy

1 tablespoon all-purpose flour

⅔ cup red wine

Serves 4

Beef in red wine
with parsley thyme dumplings

This traditional meat dish is cooked with a *bouquet garni,* the French term for a bundle of herbs. In this case, it consists of a bay leaf, thyme, and parsley, and gives extra punch to the stew. Parsley and thyme pack the dumplings full of flavor—make them with vegetable shortening for a light finish.

Dip the meat in the seasoned flour, heat the oil in a casserole dish, add the pieces of meat, and sauté until sealed and browned. Stir in the vegetables, red wine, stock, and bouquet garni. Bring to a boil, cover with a lid, place in a preheated oven, and cook at 325°F for 1 hour. Stir in the seasoning.
To make the herb dumplings, rub the vegetable shortening into the flour until it resembles fine breadcrumbs. Mix in the chopped herbs, stir in about 2 to 4 tablespoons water, and shape the mixture into small golf-ball-sized dumplings.
Place around the top of the casserole, return to the oven and cook, uncovered, for 20 to 30 minutes more, until the dumplings have risen, then serve.

1 lb. chuck steak, cubed

2 tablespoons seasoned flour

2 tablespoons olive oil

8 oz. baby onions

8 oz. baby carrots

⅔ cup red wine

1 cup vegetable stock

1 bouquet garni

salt and freshly ground black pepper

herb dumplings

2 oz. vegetable shortening

1 cup all-purpose flour

2 tablespoons chopped, fresh, flat-leaf parsley

2 teaspoons chopped fresh thyme leaves

Serves 4

a traditional dish made with **bouquet garni,**

served with **herb dumplings** to mop up the sauce

Vegetarian dishes

Herbed vegetables
with parsley pesto in a crusty loaf

Spectacular but easy to make for a casual
lunch or picnic. Try making pesto with
parsley for a refreshing change.

To make the parsley pesto, place all the ingredients
in a blender and puree to form a smooth paste.
Brush the eggplants, zucchini, and tomatoes with
olive oil and broil for 5 to 7 minutes until dark brown.
Cut the top off the loaf and hollow out the middle,
leaving a 1-inch crust. Rub the inside with the cut
sides of the garlic and drizzle with olive oil.
Spread the pesto over the base, add the arugula and
torn basil leaves, then place the vegetables inside
the loaf in layers, seasoning each layer.
Top with a spoonful of pesto and replace
the bread lid. Serve in chunky wedges.

6 oz. eggplants, sliced

6 oz. zucchini, sliced

4 plum tomatoes, halved

4–6 tablespoons
olive oil

1 loaf of crusty bread

1 large garlic clove,
cut in half

2 oz. arugula

torn leaves from
1 bunch of basil

salt and freshly
ground black pepper

parsley pesto

1 oz. parsley

1 oz. pignoli nuts

1 oz. Parmesan cheese

½ cup olive oil

Serves 4

Mini pizzas
with arugula, oregano, and olives

You can buy ready-made pizza bases, but it is always worth making your own to make sure they're light and crisp. You can also replace some of the flour with polenta grain or rye flour, and add some of the firmer herbs, such as rosemary, marjoram, or thyme. When it comes to pizza toppings— the simpler the ingredients the better.

To make the pizza dough, mash the yeast with a pinch of sugar and the warm water until creamy, then leave to rise for 20 minutes. Place the flour and salt in a large bowl, stir in the milk, olive oil, and risen yeast, and mix together to form a sticky dough. Knead the mixture to form a smooth dough (about 10 minutes), adding extra flour if necessary. Brush the surface of the dough with oil to prevent a crust forming, cover the bowl with a kitchen towel, and leave in a warm place to rise for about 2 hours. Knead again to knock all the air out of the dough, leave to rise for another 40 minutes. Divide the dough into 4 equal parts and roll into 4 small rounds. Set aside while you prepare the topping. To make the topping, scatter the arugula, herbs, and olives over the pizzas, drizzle with olive oil, then sprinkle with sea salt and black pepper. Bake in a preheated oven at 425°F for 10 to 15 minutes, or until golden. Serve with a salad of vine-ripened tomatoes and basil.

home-mad

you

izzas are a **revelation**—make them with

hoice of toppings—the **simpler the better**

pizza dough

½ oz. fresh yeast

a pinch of sugar

5 tablespoons
warm water

3 cups all-purpose
flour, organic
if possible

½ teaspoon salt

1 cup plus 1 tablespoon
warm milk

2 tablespoons olive oil,
plus extra, for brushing

oregano topping

2 oz. arugula

1 tablespoon chopped
fresh oregano leaves

1 tablespoon chopped
fresh thyme leaves

⅓ cup pitted black
olives, coated in herbs

olive oil

sea salt and freshly
ground black pepper

Serves 4

Herbed cheese calzone
with asparagus or broccoli

A calzone is a closed pizza with the filling
inside, made with the same dough as on
page 50–51, though you can also use pastry.

Divide the dough into 4 and roll out into rounds.
Mix the remaining ingredients together, divide into
4, and place on one half of each circle. Brush the
edges of the dough with water, fold over, and press
together. Fold over again, to make a firm seal. Cook
in a preheated oven at 425°F for 15 to 18 minutes
until the edges are just brown, golden, and crisp.
Serve with a herb and leaf salad.

1 batch of pizza dough
(see pages 50–51)

6 oz. goat cheese,
crumbled

6 oz. asparagus or
purple-sprouting
broccoli, blanched

1 garlic clove, crushed

2 tablespoons chopped
fresh marjoram

salt and freshly
ground black pepper

Serves 4

Tomato basil sauce
served with fresh pasta

Basil is the herb that seems just made for
tomatoes—and it's a combination that will
taste even better if you leave the tomatoes to
marinate in olive oil and balsamic vinegar.

Place the tomatoes in a saucepan, pour over the
olive oil and vinegar, add the pignoli nuts, then
season with salt and pepper. Tear the basil leaves
into pieces, add to the tomatoes, then warm through.
Cook the pasta in boiling salted water until *al dente*,
then drain and serve in pasta bowls, with the
tomatoes and basil piled on top.

8 oz. cherry
tomatoes, halved

4 tablespoons olive oil

1 tablespoon
balsamic vinegar

2 oz. pignoli nuts,
toasted

1 bunch of fresh basil

1 lb. fresh pasta

sea salt and freshly
ground black pepper

Serves 4

Marjoram frittata
with zucchini and cheese

A frittata is a chunky Italian omelet, ideal for
summer lunches, served in wedges, with a
leafy green salad. They can be made with
various ingredients, from roasted asparagus
to marinated artichokes or steamed baby
new potatoes tossed in chive butter. The
flavoring possibilities are endless!

8 eggs

2 small zucchini

4 tablespoons chopped
fresh marjoram leaves

¼ cup pecorino
romano or Parmesan
cheese, shredded

olive oil, for cooking

salt and freshly
ground black pepper

Serves 4

Break the eggs into a bowl and beat lightly with a
fork. Shred the zucchini and add to the bowl with the
marjoram and cheese.
Heat the oil in an 8-inch skillet, then add a ladle of
the egg mixture, tilt the pan to spread the mixture
then turn the heat to low.
When the frittata is set on the underside, place it
under a preheated broiler until brown.
Tip onto a plate and set aside, while you repeat with
the remaining mixture. Alternatively, use a skillet
with deeper sides and cook all the mixture at once.

Rosemary zucchini
in herb pastry crust

This pie filling mixture of summer squashes with rosemary and Parmesan can also be used as a sauce to serve with pasta.

To make the pastry, place the flour in a bowl, then mix in the remaining ingredients with a fork. Knead rapidly to form a dough, form into a ball, cover with a kitchen towel, then set aside and leave the dough to rest for about 1 hour.

To make the filling, slice and dice the zucchini and thinly slice the tomatoes. Heat the olive oil in a skillet and gently sauté the shallots for about 10 minutes. Mix the crushed garlic with the egg, stir in the zucchini and the remaining ingredients, then season with salt and pepper.

Roll out half of the pastry on a well-floured board, trim to an approximate circle, and place on a lightly oiled baking tray. Spread the filling evenly over the surface to within ¾ inch of the edge of the cirle. Roll out the remaining pastry just wider than the first, fold it and cut a tiny "V" out of the center to form a vent. Moisten the edges of the bottom round of pastry, then fold and seal the top into place, pressing all the way around with your finger. Turn the sealed edges upward and inward to form a thick roll.

Brush the surfaces with olive oil and bake in a preheated oven at 400°F for 35 to 45 minutes, until the pastry is rich and golden.

Serve warm or cold with a tomato and basil salad.

1 lb. zucchini

4 sun-dried tomatoes

2 tablespoons olive oil

2 shallots, finely sliced

2 garlic cloves, crushed

1 egg, beaten

4 sprigs of rosemary

¼ cup Parmesan cheese

⅔ cup crème fraîche

sea salt and pepper

herb pastry

2 cups flour

½ teaspoon chopped fresh oregano

¼ teaspoon chopped fresh thyme

¼ teaspoon chopped fresh rosemary leaves

1 egg

4 tablespoons olive oil

4 tablespoons water

salt

Serves 4

Chard-filled onions
with sage and Parmesan sauce

Ideal for a midweek dinner—baked onions
with a leafy filling of herbs and chard or
spinach, plus a hot béchamel sauce.

Place the unpeeled onions in a pan, cover with water
and boil, uncovered, for 10 minutes. Drain and cool.
Trim off the root and peel off the outer skins. Using
a teaspoon, hollow out the center so you are left with
2 thick layers for the shell. Chop up the insides of
the onions and reserve for later.
Place 1 teaspoon of the butter in a saucepan and
melt over a moderate heat. Add the Swiss chard,
garlic, and sage, and cook gently for 3 to 4 minutes.
Drain and squeeze out any excess moisture. Place in
a bowl and mix in the chopped onion.
To make the béchamel sauce, melt the butter, stir in
the flour, and cook for 1 minute, stirring constantly.
Gradually beat in the milk, a little at a time, then
bring to a boil and simmer until the sauce thickens.
Reserve 1 tablespoon of the Parmesan and the
toasted pignoli nuts, and mix the remainder into
the béchamel, together with the herb mixture.
Spoon the mixture into the onions and sprinkle with
the pignoli nuts and the reserved Parmesan.
Pour the stock around the onions and cook in a
preheated oven at 350°F for 20 minutes.
Serve immediately with a salad of endive and
watercress and baked potatoes with herb butter.

8 medium onions,
unpeeled

4 tablespoons
sweet butter

12 oz. Swiss chard
(silver beet) or spinach,
steamed, squeezed dry
and chopped

1 garlic clove, crushed

6 sage leaves

½ cup fresh Parmesan
cheese, grated

3 oz. pignoli nuts,
toasted and chopped

2 tablespoons chopped
fresh sage leaves

2 tablespoons chopped
fresh flat-leaf parsley

2 tablespoons olive oil

1¼ cups chicken stock

salt and pepper

béchamel sauce

2 tablespoons butter

¼ cup all-purpose flour

1 cup milk

Serves 4

Sweet things

Windfall apple pie
with lemon thyme

Apple pie is the perfect fall dessert—especially if you have an apple tree—use sweet windfalls as well as freshly picked ones. Everyone loves good-tasting apple desserts, and this is one of the best. The apples will pick up a delicious whisper of lemon thyme flavor.

To make the pastry, sift the flour into a large bowl, stir in the ground almonds, add the cubes of butter and, using a knife, cut the butter into the flour. Using your fingertips, rub the butter into the flour until it resembles fine breadcrumbs. Add 3 to 4 tablespoons ice-cold water and bind the mixture together to form a smooth dough. Chill while you prepare the apples. Place the sliced apples in a pie dish, and mix in the thyme, sugar, and water.

Roll out the pastry on a floured surface. Cut small strips of pastry and place round the pie edge, dab with a little cold water, then place the pastry lid on top. Trim off the excess pastry.

Cut a small slash in the center of the pie, then re-roll the trimmings and cut out pastry leaves. Brush the leaves with water and press onto the top of the pie. Brush milk over the top, place the pie on a baking tray, and cook in a preheated oven at 350°F for about 20 to 30 minutes until the pastry is golden and the apples cooked.

---

1 lb. apples, peeled, cored, and sliced

4 sprigs of lemon thyme

3 tablespoons sugar

2 tablespoons water

milk, for brushing

almond pastry

2 cups all-purpose flour

1 tablespoon ground almonds

½ cup sweet butter, softened and cut into cubes

ice-cold water (see method)

Serves 4

Citron pie
with rosemary pastry

Sift the flour and half the confectioners sugar together. Soften the butter, then rub it into the flour, with the rosemary. Add the egg yolk and enough cold water to bind the mixture. Chill for 30 minutes. Roll out the pastry and use to line a 9-inch pie dish. Prick with a fork, line with waxed paper and fill with baking beans. Bake at 400°F for 10 minutes. Remove beans and paper and cook for 10 minutes more. To make the filling, whisk the eggs with the sugar until pale, then add the lemon juice, zest, and cream. Pour into the pastry case and bake at 300°F for 30 minutes until set. Sprinkle with the remaining confectioners sugar and serve.

2 cups all-purpose flour

2 tablespoons confectioners sugar

½ cup sweet butter

1 teaspoon chopped fresh rosemary

1 egg yolk

citron filling

3 eggs

¾ cup sugar

juice and grated zest of 3 lemons

⅔ cup heavy cream

Serves 4

Lavender cookies

To make lavender sugar, place 8 to 12 blossoms in a jar of sugar and leave for 2 weeks.

Rub the butter into the flour until it resembles fine breadcrumbs. Add the sugar, lavender, and vanilla and knead to a smooth dough. Roll out on a floured surface and cut into rounds with a cookie cutter. Place on a greased baking tray in a preheated oven at 400°F for 8 to 10 minutes until golden. Cool for 2 minutes, then transfer to a wire rack. Decorate with drizzles of melted chocolate, then serve.

4 tablespoons butter

1½ cups all-purpose flour

6 tablespoons sugar or lavender sugar

1 teaspoon dried lavender, chopped

2 drops vanilla extract

2 oz. semisweet chocolate, melted

Serves 4

two unusual baking recipes, packed with **herb** flavors

Index